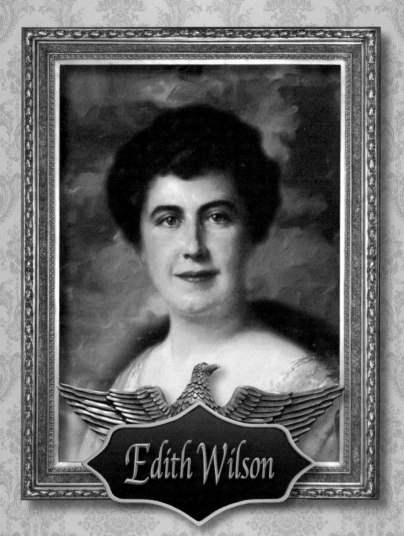

Edith Wilson

by PeggySue Wells

FIRST LADIES ⚊ SECOND TO NONE

PURPLE TOAD
PUBLISHING

FIRST LADIES **SECOND TO NONE**

Abigail Adams
Dolley Madison
Edith Wilson
Eleanor Roosevelt
Hillary Rodham Clinton
Mary Todd Lincoln

Copyright © 2016 by Purple Toad Publishing, Inc.

All rights reserved. No part of this book may be reproduced without written permission from the publisher. Printed and bound in the United States of America.

PUBLISHER'S NOTE: The data in this book has been researched in depth, and to the best of our knowledge is factual. Although every measure is taken to give an accurate account, Purple Toad Publishing makes no warranty of the accuracy of the information and is not liable for damages caused by inaccuracies.

The sidebar stories contain fictional conversation based on what historical documents suggest might have been said.

Printing 1 2 3 4 5 6 7 8 9

Publisher's Cataloging-in-Publication Data
Wells, PeggySue.
  Edith Wilson / written by PeggySue Wells.
   p. cm.
          Includes bibliographic references and index.
          ISBN 9781624691805
1. Wilson, Edith Bolling Galt, 1872-1961—Juvenile literature. 2. Wilson, Woodrow, 1856-1924—Juvenile literature. 3. Presidents' spouses—United States—Biography—Juvenile literature. I. Series: First Ladies : Second to None.
  E767.3 2016
  973.913092
Library of Congress Control Number: 2015941826
eBook ISBN: 9781624691812

Contents

Chapter One
BISHOPS
AND BOOKS

"Come here, child," the Episcopal bishop said, inviting young Edith Bolling into his office.

Edith glanced up at her father.

"Go ahead." William Holcombe Bolling patted his daughter's shoulder.

Edith followed the tall church leader. Nine years old, she was small for her age and felt even smaller in this room that smelled of furniture polish and books. Why did the leader of the Episcopal Church in Wytheville want to speak with her?

Like her siblings, Edith had been baptized at St. John's Episcopal Church. Down the street from the Bollings' home, St. John's was a familiar part of Edith's week. This meeting, though, was out of the ordinary.

The bishop lifted her onto his lap. "I believe, young lady, that you are too young and surely unprepared for catechism class."

Along with her 14-year-old brother, Edith's name had been placed on the list for confirmation. To prove his concerns, the bishop asked Edith a question. Edith answered correctly. She watched the man's bushy eyebrows rise in surprise as she correctly answered more questions about their faith. In groups of three, Edith's father had taught his children the foundations of

Strong and opinionated, Edith Bolling Wilson was First Lady to the 28th President. In 1917, she was invited to be the first Honorary President of the Girl Scouts. Since then, it has become a tradition for the First Lady to be Honorary President of the Girl Scouts.

St. John's Episcopal Church was a regular part of Edith's childhood. Established in 1845, it is a national landmark.

their religion. When older brother Will was preparing for confirmation, Edith learned alongside him.

At the end of the interview, the bishop set Edith on her feet. "Tell your father, little girl, that you are the best prepared candidate I have interviewed and I want you in that class tomorrow."[1]

The bishop knew Edith would do well in his class. What he couldn't know then was that bright young Edith would eventually become First Lady of the United States.

Family Roots

The seventh of eleven children, Edith Bolling was born October 15, 1872, in Wytheville, Virginia, to William Holcombe Bolling and Sallie White Bolling. In those days it was said that the seventh child was destined for an important life. "There is a tradition regarding the seventh child, and I suppose like other traditions, it varies," Edith wrote in her memoir. "But certainly it brought me luck and deep happiness."[2]

Edith came from a famous family. She was a descendant of the Powhatan Indian woman Matoaka, who was known as Pocahontas. She was

Edith was a descendant of the Powhatan woman Matoaka. Legend calls her Pocahontas and credits her with saving the life of Jamestown colonist John Smith.

also related to George Washington's wife, Martha Washington, Confederate General Robert E. Lee, and former First Lady Letitia Tyler. Edith's great-great-grandmother was a sister of President Thomas Jefferson.

Before the Civil War, Edith's grandparents, Archibald Bolling, Jr., and his wife, Anne Wigginton Bolling, owned a prosperous plantation in eastern Virginia. The Bolling plantation depended on cheap slave labor. Before antislavery president Abraham Lincoln took office in March 1861, seven Southern states had seceded from—or left—the United States. They became the Confederate States of America. Virginia joined them on April 17. The Civil War waged fierce throughout Virginia, and the

Founding Father and United States President Thomas Jefferson was a prominent name in Edith's family tree.

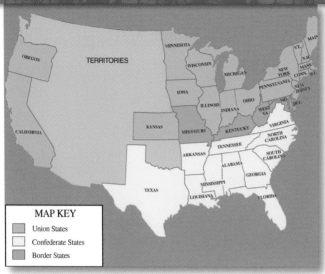

MAP KEY
- Union States
- Confederate States
- Border States

The Civil War was fought over the right of the Southern states to secede from the United States of America.

Bollings became strong supporters of the Confederate Army. Edith's mother, grandmother, and aunts opened the plantation home as a hospital during the war. They tended the wounded themselves.[3]

The Civil War destroyed the Bollings' life of "slaves and abundance."[4] Many slaves stayed on, even after the Emancipation Proclamation freed them. They had nowhere else to go, and the Bollings did not have the money to hire them. Soon the plantation could no longer support its residents. Edith remembered her father telling of the day he had no food for the former slaves or for his own family. The Union army had taken the Bollings' horses, so William drove the mule-pulled wagon to the store in Lynchburg. There, the Northern gentleman in charge generously loaded William's cart with bacon, coffee, flour, and sugar.[5]

Back home, William coaxed his wife, mother, and sister to at least have some real coffee. But the steadfast women refused anything from the Yankees.[6]

Along with his wife, two babies, and an invalid mother, William left the plantation and moved to Wytheville. Earlier, William's father had come to own a two-story building in exchange for a debt.[7] When he died, Archibald left the brick house on Main Street to his wife and William. A graduate of the University of Virginia School of Law, William planned to settle in town and build a law business to support his family. But when they arrived, they found the house in shambles. It, too, had served as a Confederate hospital before it was abandoned.[8]

Full House

The Bollings set to work, and soon 145 E. Main Street stood tidy and welcoming. Initially home to the Farmers Bank of Virginia, the house had three storefronts for

So many soldiers were wounded during the civil war, there were not enough hospitals to treat them all. Civilians acted as nurses in many plantation homes.

businesses on the first floor. The family lived on the upper floor. Young Edith remembered her father working many hours in his study, next to her parents' bedroom, with its packed bookshelves and a round-arched

The Blue Ridge Mountains are part of the Appalachian Range.

doorway that opened onto a balcony. She could see the foothills of the scenic Blue Ridge Mountains from her back porch.

In addition to their first two children, Rolfe and Gertrude, William and Sallie welcomed nine more children in Wytheville—Annie Lee, William, Bertha, Charles, Edith, John Randolph, Richard Wilmer, Julian, and Geraldine. (Charles and Geraldine died before they were two.) Edith was born in her parents' front corner bedroom on the east side[9] on October 15, 1872, at 9:00 a.m. Court came to order late that day because her father, a circuit judge by then, remained at home to greet his baby girl.[10]

Edith's home overflowed with generations of family. Two grandmothers, an aunt or two, cousin Randolph, a freed slave, an occasional border, frequent visitors, dogs, and Grandma Anne Bolling's twenty-six canaries all squeezed in with William, Sallie, and their children. With so many to feed, the family lived modestly. Grandma Bolling and Edith's mother made the clothes their large family wore. Edith recalled, "Though the house was shabby and inadequate, material deficiencies were repaired by understanding, sympathy and love, making it to us healthy, happy youngsters in every sense a home."[11]

Wytheville had no public school. Unable to afford private tutors, the Bolling children were taught at home. Edith learned to read, write, speak French, and study the Bible from Grandma Bolling. Stooped from an injury when she was thrown from a horse, Grandma Bolling was small, thin, and sharp-tongued. She dressed in black with full skirts made from six widths of fabric. "I hate a 'can't,' " she often said. "Anyone can do anything they try to."[12]

Edith's favorite place was Grandma Bolling's bedroom. In the center of the house, the spacious room held a four-poster bed with a trundle where Edith often slept. Near the fireplace was a rocking chair covered with a tanned and preserved skin from a dog that the woman had loved.[13] The elderly lady rarely left the house, and it was Edith's job to tell her grandmother what was happening in the world outside the busy Bolling household.

Busy Birds

"Here is flannel for the birds." Grandma Bolling handed Edith some scraps from the suit she was making.

Edith climbed on a stool to see inside the busy cage. The twenty-six canaries reminded Edith of her own busy household, filled to the rafters with ten children and various relatives. Lining a nest with the soft cloth, Edith noticed a baby bird on the bottom of the cage.

"Poor thing." Edith scooped the lifeless body into a spool box and called for her brother William. He was deciding between becoming a priest or a doctor when he was grown.

"It appears we are too late to save the patient." Will made his voice deep like an adult's. "Since we can't cure the bird, it seems a funeral is necessary."

Will carried the box outside and placed it in a trusty wagon. Attempting the solemnity of a funeral procession, Will and Edith pulled the wagon to a bright spot in the garden near the stable. Will dug a hole and Edith laid the box in the resting place.

Will led a brief ceremony, trying to look serious while Edith suppressed smiles. They wrote the date on a stone chip and laid it on the miniature grave.

"Edith! Will!" Grandma Bolling called.

"She is ready to fit the jacket to you," Edith said. "And there will be more scraps for the birds."

The siblings grinned. Will grabbed the wagon handle, and the two raced each other back to the house.

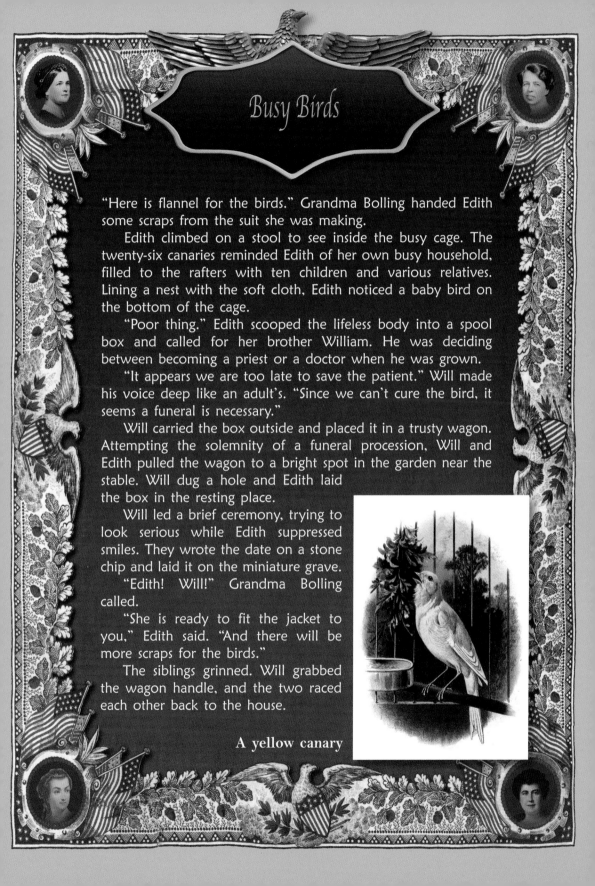

A yellow canary

Chapter Two
STORIES AND CARS

Gathered around the hearth in the evenings, Edith's family shared stories of the Civil War. Edith's favorite was the one her father told about his business partner, Confederate General William Terry. Though she had heard it many times, Edith never tired of hearing how her father had outrun the Union Army.

At age 15, Edith attended Martha Washington College to study music. A Scrooge-like man, the schoolmaster barely fed students and refused to heat their rooms or practice studios. Hungry and with fingers often too cold to play, Edith diligently worked on her studies. She returned home thin, but had become a beautiful young woman who was five feet nine inches tall.[1]

Edith remained at home for a year to recover her strength before attending Edith Powell's School in Richmond. Her father could only afford the small private school for so long. In those days it was considered more important for sons to receive a high school and college education than daughters. Edith's formal education stopped so that her three younger brothers could go to school.

Edith's childhood home in Wytheville appears much as it did when Edith lived there. The museum houses the family's antique child rocker and cradle, furniture, books, letters, paintings, and photographs of Edith.

The next winter, Edith went to Washington, D.C., to stay with her sister Gertrude for four months. Gertrude's husband introduced her to his cousin, Norman Galt, who fell madly in love with Edith.

Galt had a bright future ahead of him. At only 27 years old, he already owned a family jewelry business. He sent Edith flowers and candy, visiting her often in Washington and later in Virginia to try to win her heart. Edith was used to attention. It took her a year to realize that his feelings for her were more than friendship.

Edith knew that she was expected to marry, and though she never said she loved Norman, she wrote, "We were the best of friends and I liked him immensely." After four years of what Edith described as "close and delightful friendship," she accepted his proposal.[2]

They were married in 1896, and Edith set up housekeeping in their small Washington home the day before Thanksgiving. She wasted no time in making her new husband feel a part of her big, beloved family. "All my family was devoted to Norman," Edith said, "and no one could have been lovelier than he to each and every one of them. He was sound in his judgments and unfailing in his eagerness to help the younger boys and do anything he could for anyone I loved."[3]

In 1899, the newlyweds experienced overwhelming loss. Norman's brother-in-law died, and within 24 hours, Norman's father died. Norman was left in charge of the 100-year-old Galt jewelry business.[4] Soon after, Norman's unmarried brother, Charlie, took so ill that he became an invalid, needing constant care. That same year, Edith's beloved Grandmother Bolling died, and then her father.

Deeply missing her father and grandmother, Edith traveled to Wytheville to help sell the family home. Eventually her mother, Sallie, and three brothers moved to Washington, where her brothers worked in the Galt jewelry business.

Loss gave way to joy in 1903. Edith and Norman were expecting their first child. But when Edith gave birth to their son, the baby lived only three days. Her family physician, Dr. Cary Grayson, cared for Edith through her recovery. He told her she would not be able to have more children. This

From her first husband, Edith inherited the Galt Jewelry Store, a popular place for Washington, D.C.'s high society to shop.

loss was so profound that Edith never wrote or spoke about her son again, and few people ever knew that part of her life.

In 1908, Norman, too, fell ill and died, leaving Edith a widow and in charge of the jewelry business. The store provided much-needed income for Edith, her mother, three brothers, and an unmarried sister. Some employees, too, had been with the company for nearly 30 years. Edith knew little about operating a company, but she was determined to see it through. To prepare for the task, she asked Henry Bergheimer, the manager who had served both Norman and her father-in-law, to teach her what she needed to know. Edith and Bergheimer both took meager salaries until the debts were repaid.

Edith Bolling Galt was the first woman in Washington, D.C., to own an electric car.

Soon Edith was going over accounts and making decisions for the future of the store. The business did so well that Edith became the first woman in Washington to own an electric automobile when cars were still new and rare on the streets.[5] Every year, Edith and a woman friend vacationed in Europe. There, Edith acquired a stunning spring and fall wardrobe from the renowned Paris designer Monsieur Worth.[6] Well-dressed and successful, she was enjoying the theater and opera in France when Woodrow Wilson was elected 28th President of the United States.

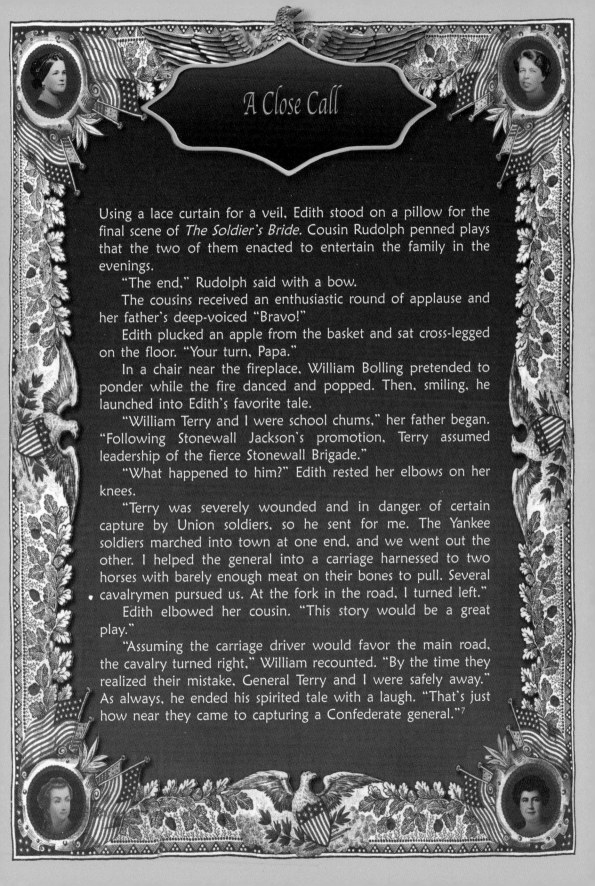

Using a lace curtain for a veil, Edith stood on a pillow for the final scene of *The Soldier's Bride*. Cousin Rudolph penned plays that the two of them enacted to entertain the family in the evenings.

"The end," Rudolph said with a bow.

The cousins received an enthusiastic round of applause and her father's deep-voiced "Bravo!"

Edith plucked an apple from the basket and sat cross-legged on the floor. "Your turn, Papa."

In a chair near the fireplace, William Bolling pretended to ponder while the fire danced and popped. Then, smiling, he launched into Edith's favorite tale.

"William Terry and I were school chums," her father began. "Following Stonewall Jackson's promotion, Terry assumed leadership of the fierce Stonewall Brigade."

"What happened to him?" Edith rested her elbows on her knees.

"Terry was severely wounded and in danger of certain capture by Union soldiers, so he sent for me. The Yankee soldiers marched into town at one end, and we went out the other. I helped the general into a carriage harnessed to two horses with barely enough meat on their bones to pull. Several cavalrymen pursued us. At the fork in the road, I turned left."

Edith elbowed her cousin. "This story would be a great play."

"Assuming the carriage driver would favor the main road, the cavalry turned right," William recounted. "By the time they realized their mistake, General Terry and I were safely away." As always, he ended his spirited tale with a laugh. "That's just how near they came to capturing a Confederate general."[7]

Chapter Three
MUDDY SHOES AND MARRIAGE

The day of the Inaugural Parade was bright with American flags. Crowds of excited people lined the streets of Washington, D.C., to catch a glimpse of President Woodrow Wilson and his wife, Ellen, and welcome them to the White House. Edith passed on the chance to view the parade from the Galt store balcony. She visited her mother instead. A Southern widow of reduced circumstances, Sallie lived at Washington's Powhatan Hotel. Edith wasn't a political person but read a volume of Wilson's speeches. He had big plans for the country. She wondered how he would achieve them.

The next night, Edith and a relative went to a play at the National Theatre. Though it starred the famous actress Billie Burke, the curious Edith was more interested in seeing the new president, rumored to also be in the audience. Sure enough, the President and Ellen Wilson sat in box seats just above her. Edith watched the President yawn several times. Was he bored with the performance? Or exhausted after the events of recent days? Through her friend, Dr. Grayson, Edith knew that on Inauguration Day, the president's sister had gashed her head. The naval doctor had saved the day and gained the confidence of the Wilson family.[1]

Woodrow and his first wife, Ellen Axson, had three daughters: Margaret, Jessie, and Eleanor.

A surgeon with the U.S. Navy, Admiral Cary Traverse Grayson was physician to the President and longtime friend to Edith. Grayson introduced widow Edith Bolling Galt to widower Woodrow Wilson.

With talk of war overseas in 1914, Edith vacationed in Maine with a new young friend. An admirer of Edith's, Scottish millionaire James Gordon, had recently lost his wife. He introduced Edith to his daughter. Edith and Alice Gertrude Gordon, better known as Altrude, became fast friends. Edith introduced Altrude to Dr. Grayson, and the two were dating.

Altrude and Edith expected Dr. Grayson to join them in Maine that summer, but Dr. Grayson remained in Washington, treating the president's wife. Seriously ill from kidney failure, Ellen Wilson died in August. Woodrow had deeply loved Ellen. He confided in her and relied on her opinions. Even the President's cabinet prized her insights and clear thinking in political matters. Now, so soon after Ellen's death, the grief-stricken president was under more pressure than ever as war broke out in Europe. Dr. Grayson stayed close to the nation's leader to look after his health.

Woodrow Wilson

"Turn a corner, meet your fate,"[2] Edith wrote about her chance meeting with President Wilson. He invited Edith to dinners at the White House. Accompanied by his cousin Helen Bones, the President took Edith on afternoon drives. Wilson continued a precedent set by President William Howard Taft of throwing the first baseball of the season, and he and Edith attended games together. With friends, he and Edith sailed the Potomac River and Chesapeake Bay aboard the presidential yachts, the *Sylph* and the *Mayflower*. Discovering her favorite flower, Woodrow daily sent Edith an orchid.

President Wilson took Edith to the ballgame where he threw out the first ball of the 1915 World Series.

At 58 years old, Woodrow had energy and drive to match Edith, who was 42.

By May, Woodrow told Edith he loved her.

"Oh, you can't love me," Edith replied. "You don't really know me and it's less than a year since your wife died."

Edith Bolling Galt

Wilson was sincere. "But, little girl, in this place, time is not measured by weeks, or months, or years, but by deep human experience; and since her death I have lived a lifetime of loneliness and heartache. I was afraid, knowing you, I would shock you but I would be less than a gentleman if I continued to make opportunities to see you without telling you . . . that I want you to be my wife."[3]

In a storybook courtship, Edith and Woodrow saw each other through the summer of 1915 and exchanged letters when they were apart. As he had done with his first wife, the President took Edith into his confidence. His letters were filled with romance and his concerns of state, including the tensions in Europe that could lead to war.

In one of her letters to him, Edith wrote, "Much as I enjoy your delicious love letters, I believe I enjoy even more the ones in which you tell me what you are working on—the things that fill your thoughts and demand your best effort. For

The May 1915 sinking of the passenger ship *Lusitania* by the Germans was an act of war.

then I feel I am sharing your work and being taken into partnership, as it were."[4]

When President Wilson drafted a letter to the Germans protesting the sinking of the British luxury liner *Lusitania,* Edith encouraged him to strengthen the message on behalf of the 128 Americans who died.

In September, Woodrow asked Edith to marry him and she accepted. Members of his cabinet as well as Wilson's close friend, Colonel Edward M. House, and his loyal private secretary, Joseph Tumulty, were concerned. They warned him that this

The press and the American public embraced the romance between Edith and Woodrow.

romance so quickly after Ellen's death would look bad to voters. It could harm his reelection campaign.[5]

In October the press announced their engagement. On December 18, 1915, nine months after they met, the two were wed at Edith's home. Only family members of the bride and groom attended the wedding. Edith wore a black velvet dress and hat. To go with her outfit was a large diamond pin and spray of white orchids from her groom. The President wore a cutaway coat and gray-striped trousers. The wedding band he slipped onto Edith's finger was fashioned from a gold nugget from the oldest mine in California.

The newlyweds took a two-week honeymoon to Hot Springs, Virginia.[6]

Mere months after meeting, Edith and Woodrow were married in a small ceremony at her home surrounded by family and close friends.

Tea for Two?

Dr. Grayson was worried about Ellen Wilson's personal assistant, Helen Bones. A cousin of Woodrow's, Helen was devastated by the loss of her boss.

"It would be a kindness if you would walk with her," Dr. Grayson suggested to Edith. "The exercise in the fresh air, as well as your friendship, will lift her spirits."

Edith agreed. In March, Helen picked up Edith in a White House car and drove to the park. Helen spoke of missing Ellen as well as the effect the loss of his wife had on President Wilson. She described Woodrow as a man of intelligence, integrity, and character.

After their walk, Helen invited Edith back to the White House for tea.

"Oh, I couldn't." Edith eyed the mud caked on her shoes.

Helen waved away her concerns. "No one will see your shoes. The President is out golfing with Dr. Grayson."

Although hesitant, Edith agreed.

When the elevator door opened to the second floor of the White House, the two women saw the two men, who had just returned from their golf game. Edith's eyes went to their shoes, which were even muddier than hers. At least, Edith comforted herself, she was stylishly dressed in an outfit by European designer Monsieur Worth.[7]

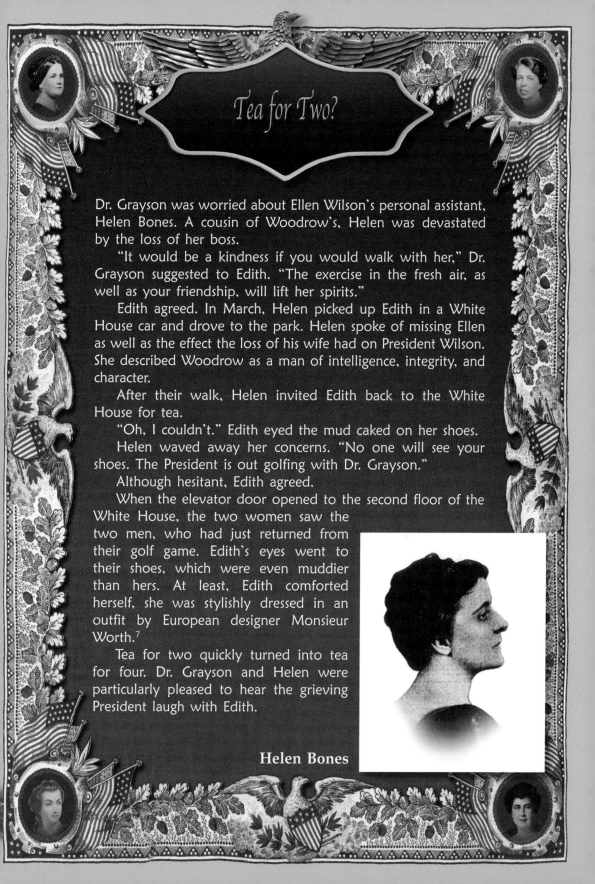

Tea for two quickly turned into tea for four. Dr. Grayson and Helen were particularly pleased to hear the grieving President laugh with Edith.

Helen Bones

Chapter Four
WILSON'S SECOND FIRST LADY

Edith was the first First Lady to ride with her husband to and from his swearing-in ceremony. A month later, on April 2, 1917, Edith watched from the Capitol gallery as President Wilson addressed Congress. Crowded into the gallery were 1,500 special guests and members of the press. Below the gallery, the floor was filled with members of the Senate, House of Representatives, Supreme Court, President's Cabinet, diplomatic corps, and foreign envoys.

Since the war began in 1914, President Wilson had remained neutral on the European war. But the United States took a stand when German submarines sank American passenger and merchant vessels. Germany had also promised Mexico that if Mexico fought with Germany, it could have the land it had lost to the United States after the Mexican-American War. "The world must be made safe for democracy," Wilson said. "We desire no conquest, no dominion . . . But we are one of the champions of the rights of mankind."[1]

All three branches of government stood and applauded as the President left the podium. Edith descended from the gallery to meet him. The couple

On April 2, 1917, Edith watched from the packed gallery as President Wilson asked Congress to declare war.

rode to the White House in silence, overwhelmed by this serious step that would cost American lives.

The nation plunged into the long-avoided war. The First Lady canceled public tours of the White House, the annual Easter Egg Roll, the New Year's Day reception, and most formal dinners. A role model as a U.S. citizen, Edith scheduled gasless Sundays, meatless Mondays, and wheatless Wednesdays at the presidential mansion. She wore secondhand clothes from thrift stores as the government asked Americans to save precious resources to support the nation's army of four million men. Edith joined the Red Cross and knit liners for trench helmets. She also sewed pajamas, pillowcases, and blankets. She promoted war bonds, responded to soldiers' mail, and named thousands of ships.[2]

The press called Edith "the shepherdess" when she borrowed a small herd of sheep to graze the White House lawn rather than employ a gardening crew. The

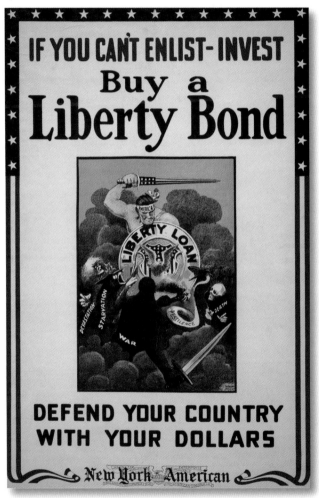

Edith championed the sale of war bonds to raise funds for the American military.

Dubbed "the shepherdess" by the press, Edith grazed a small herd of sheep on the White House lawn and sold the fleece to support the Red Cross.

sheep were shorn and the wool was sold. The money it earned was donated to the war effort.[3]

Ever her husband's trusted partner, Edith learned a private war code. She worked into the night decoding messages and helping President Wilson compose coded messages to the leaders of other nations. When President Wilson was too busy for visitors, she substituted for him by meeting with guests.

Edith remembered the two men in the President's confidence who had opposed their marriage. She recommended to her husband that Colonel House and Private Secretary Tumulty be let go.[4] Though President Wilson did not follow her suggestion, it was obvious that Edith had a great deal of influence over him.

At 3:00 a.m. on November 11, 1918, the President received a cablegram stating that the war was over. Edith and President Wilson were elated by the news, but they grieved the 116,516 brave American soldiers who had died, with 204,002 more wounded and 4,500 missing.[5]

War Takes Its Toll

No president had traveled out of the country during his term in office, but President Wilson believed he should go to Paris to help write the treaty. He believed world peace should be the foundation of the treaty when the Allies met to discuss peace terms. He envisioned a League of Nations, in which countries would work together to protect against another world war. The President's advisers told him he should not go. Edith argued that he should.

Edith boarded the *George Washington* with him. Overseas, she made appearances with the President and shopped. Always a snappy dresser, she caught the attention of the press with her stylish hats and scarves. Her presence among the European queens and aristocracy made America's First Lady look to other nations like royalty. To a British nobleman, Edith said the only reason she didn't wear a tiara was because she didn't own one.[6]

President Wilson and Edith thanked troops, toured war-ravaged Rheims, and visited the wounded. "I felt so ashamed," Edith said. "There they were, some with their entire noses blown away, some totally blind, others with chins and half their faces gone. . . . [I] told them how proud I was just to touch their hands."[7]

Edith did not participate in the peace treaty discussions, but each evening her husband recounted the day's events. By February 14, she didn't want to just hear about events. She wanted to be there when her husband presented his League of Nations to the peace conference.

Only commission members were allowed to attend, but Edith asked the conference president to make an exception for her. The only woman in attendance, and hidden behind heavy curtains in the Hall of Mirrors, Edith stood for five hours to see peace conference delegates approve and sign the treaty.[8] The Wilsons sailed home to secure approval from the U.S. Senate for the treaty, which included the President's bold plans for the League of Nations.

Opposition

Some in Congress thought the United States would lose its independence if it joined the League of Nations. They also did not believe American soldiers should have to defend other countries. Led by Henry Cabot Lodge of Massachusetts, 38 Republican Senators opposed the plan. Edith and the President sailed back to France and lobbied the peace conference delegates to make changes.

Edith knew her husband would not be content with a peace treaty that did not safeguard against another world war, but she became concerned for his wellbeing. Woodrow's health had always been fragile, and pressures of the presidency would be wearing on even the healthiest of men. Dr. Grayson had prescribed a healthy diet and a daily walk for fresh air. But the President became increasingly driven. Even when he was sick with the flu, he worked long and hard to get the League of Nations approved.

The peace treaty was signed at last on June 28, 1919, in the Hall of Mirrors at Versailles. Their goal accomplished, the Wilsons returned home, where President Wilson presented the treaty to the U.S. Senate. Representing the people of the United States, President Wilson had already signed the treaty. But many senators still opposed the League of Nations. Wilson refused to break his word, imploring

In Europe, President Wilson conferred with England's Prime Minister David Lloyd George, Italian Premier Vittorio Orlando, and French Premier Georges Clemenceau to discuss world peace.

Despite Edith's growing concerns for his health, President Wilson embarked on a cross-country campaign for the League of Nations.

the Senators, "Dare we reject it and break the heart of the world?"[9]

Edith was alarmed when Wilson decided to make a cross-country railroad tour to gain support for the League of Nations. She knew her husband was exhausted. She and Dr. Grayson tried to talk him out of the trip, but President Wilson's desire for world peace was unflappable.

In September's oppressive heat, the president's special train left Washington's Union Station for a 10,000-mile cross-country tour. Aboard were the Wilsons, Dr. Grayson, presidential assistants, Secret Service men, and reporters.

Traveling through two states a day, at each stop the President spoke about the value of the League of Nations. It was a grueling trip following two transatlantic voyages, in addition to his hard work to spark cooperation among world leaders. Worse yet, Wilson's opponents traveled hot on his heels, arguing against participation in the League of Nations.

Edith watched her husband become increasingly weary. She urged him to rest but President Wilson refused to slow down. In Pueblo, Colorado, Edith became anxious when the President stumbled for words during his speech. Recently his headaches had intensified. The morning after his halting speech in Pueblo, one side of the President's face drooped and his words slurred. Dr. Grayson and Edith insisted the President rest. The tour was canceled and the train raced back to Washington, D.C.

The morning of October 2, Woodrow lost feeling in his left hand and was in tremendous pain. After summoning Dr. Grayson, Edith returned to find her husband on the floor, unconscious. When he came to, the left side of his body was paralyzed, and he was blind in his left eye. Dr. Grayson confirmed that the President had suffered a severe stroke.

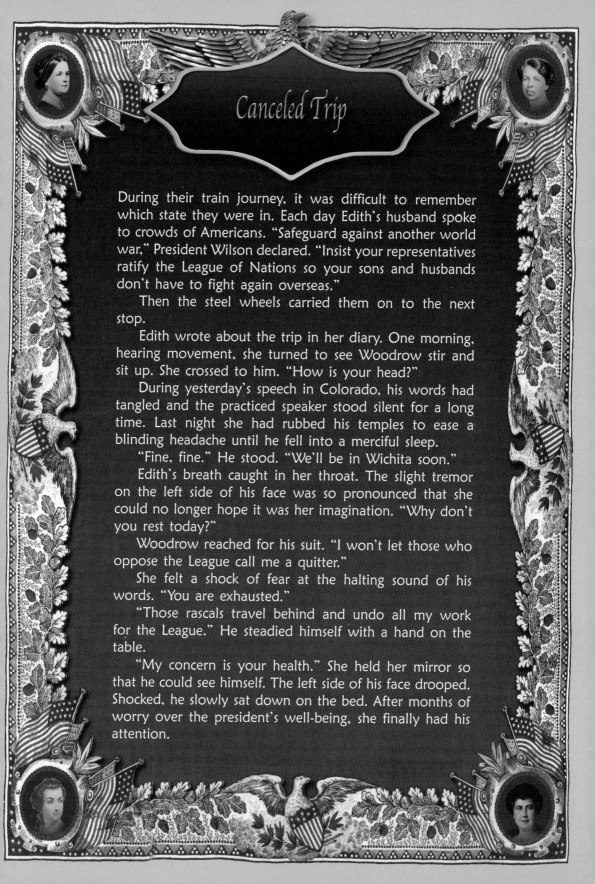

Canceled Trip

During their train journey, it was difficult to remember which state they were in. Each day Edith's husband spoke to crowds of Americans. "Safeguard against another world war," President Wilson declared. "Insist your representatives ratify the League of Nations so your sons and husbands don't have to fight again overseas."

Then the steel wheels carried them on to the next stop.

Edith wrote about the trip in her diary. One morning, hearing movement, she turned to see Woodrow stir and sit up. She crossed to him. "How is your head?"

During yesterday's speech in Colorado, his words had tangled and the practiced speaker stood silent for a long time. Last night she had rubbed his temples to ease a blinding headache until he fell into a merciful sleep.

"Fine, fine." He stood. "We'll be in Wichita soon."

Edith's breath caught in her throat. The slight tremor on the left side of his face was so pronounced that she could no longer hope it was her imagination. "Why don't you rest today?"

Woodrow reached for his suit. "I won't let those who oppose the League call me a quitter."

She felt a shock of fear at the halting sound of his words. "You are exhausted."

"Those rascals travel behind and undo all my work for the League." He steadied himself with a hand on the table.

"My concern is your health." She held her mirror so that he could see himself. The left side of his face drooped. Shocked, he slowly sat down on the bed. After months of worry over the president's well-being, she finally had his attention.

Chapter Five
MRS. PRESIDENT?

Dr. Grayson told reporters the President was very ill, but he did not mention the stroke. After some days it became apparent that while the President was physically limited, his brain remained unaffected. Their only hope of recovery was complete rest.

With 18 months left to his term, the President was protected from anything and anyone that did not first go through Edith. She decided what the President saw and what he did not. What she did not give to him, she gave to the heads of departments. Edith considered this critical period as her "stewardship." Her critics called her the "secret president" and "first woman to run the government." [1] They believed she was acting as a policy maker and decision maker.

"I, myself, never made a single decision regarding . . . public affairs," she wrote in her memoir. "The only decision that was mine was what was important to what was not, and the *very* important decision of when to present matters to my husband."[2]

From October 1919 to April 1920—a period sometimes referred to as Edith's regency—the First Lady was the gatekeeper between the recovering President and the rest of the world. Working late into the night, she

Edith was Woodrow's constant companion, carefully screening items of business and visitors to allow the President to rest and recover.

painstakingly went over the papers intended for the President. Deciphering her husband's rough speech, she made copious notes and relayed his responses.

Edith was not above refusing to allow Colonel House and Private Secretary Tumulty to visit the President. She had not forgotten that House and Tumulty had not readily approved her marriage. Now, years later, Edith was in a position to make decisions affecting these two men. Likewise, she refused to acknowledge the British ambassador, Lord Grey, who had come from England to help President Wilson secure Senate acceptance of the League of Nations. An aide of Grey's had made comments about her that she did not like. She insisted Grey send his aide back to England; otherwise, he would not be granted an audience with the President. Grey returned to England without seeing or helping the President.[3]

In January, the President was well enough to move about in a wheelchair. Edith frequently translated his slurred speech. On January 10, 1920, the League of Nations was founded. The mission of the global organization was to secure world peace. The Wilsons were delighted that Europe had embraced the League of Nations. But the U.S. Senate never approved America's membership in the League.[4]

Political cartoons noted that while 58 nations were members of Wilson's League of Nations, the United States never joined.

Keeper of the Flame

On Election Day in 1920, Warren G. Harding won by a landslide. Edith and Woodrow retired to a comfortable home in Washington in 1921. They watched movies in their library, took automobile rides as they had when they'd courted, and visited Woodrow's daughters and their families. Woodrow considered writing a book. He composed the opening, dedicating the book to Edith, but never wrote any more on the project. Three years later, on February 3, 1924, Edith's famous husband died.

When Edith heard that Henry Cabot Lodge had been invited to President Wilson's funeral at Washington's National Cathedral, she wrote to advise him not to attend. Edith believed Lodge's opposition to the League of Nations had largely caused her husband's stroke. Woodrow had never been the same, and Edith could not forget.

President Wilson was awarded the 1919 Nobel Peace Prize for his efforts in founding the League of Nations. He received the prize one year later.

Edith dedicated the rest of her life to promoting the legacy of President Woodrow Wilson. She worked tirelessly toward the founding of the Woodrow Wilson Presidential Library and Museum at his boyhood home in Staunton, Virginia. She supplied letters and papers to authors who wrote biographies about him. As she had protected her husband during his illness, she was the gateway for who received access to his papers. She would allow only those who would portray her husband in a favorable light to see her carefully cared-for resources.

For 37 years after Woodrow died, Edith stayed in their Washington home and remained a highly respected public figure. Outgoing First Lady Edith Wilson and incoming First Lady Florence Harding set a new precedent when they rode together to Harding's inauguration.[5] When President Franklin D. Roosevelt asked Congress to declare war on Japan, he asked Edith to sit in the gallery with his wife, Eleanor, as Edith had done when President Wilson had asked for war in 1917.

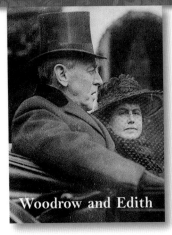

Woodrow and Edith

A lifelong supporter of the Red Cross, Edith once more sewed for the war effort. At the end of World War II in 1945, the United Nations was organized. President Wilson was recognized during the founding ceremonies.

Edith returned to her hometown of Wytheville in 1960 to dedicate a stained glass window at St. John's Episcopal Church in memory of her parents. It would be her last visit to the town where she was born, baptized, and married to her first husband. She recalled the day years before when the bishop had been surprised at how prepared she was for catechism class. Reflecting on her childhood, brief school career, and period as a business owner, Edith knew each experience had prepared her for her future as First Lady of the United States.

When she was 88 years old, Edith rode in an open car for the January 20, 1961, inaugural parade for President John F. Kennedy. Though her health had begun to fail in November, Edith planned to attend a dedication of the Woodrow Wilson Bridge over the Potomac River. It would be held on December 28, the 105th anniversary of President Wilson's birth. But early that morning, she died peacefully in her sleep.

Edith was buried near President Wilson at the National Cathedral, the only presidential couple buried in Washington, D.C. In her will, she left their modest home on S Street to the National Trust for Historic Preservation. Today it houses a museum honoring President Wilson.

Interestingly, it was Edith's role and legacy as a wife that attracted criticism. In an era when women had yet to vote, Edith opposed letting women vote. She supported her husband's presidency through her organizational skills, quick mind, and courage. Her strength and experience prepared her for the months when President Wilson was bedridden.

Whether Edith acted as president while her husband was partly paralyzed is still questioned. Fresh laws were enacted to prevent similar situations. The unusual circumstances made Edith Bolling Galt Wilson one of the most controversial women in American history.

Stepping into Stewardship

Satisfied that her husband was resting, Edith allowed Dr. Grayson to lead her from the President's bedroom. Giving orders for strong tea, he sent everyone else away.

"What is my husband's condition?" Taking a chair near his, she kept her voice low.

The doctor sighed. "It is a grave situation, but I think you can save it."

"Me? How can that be?" Her hand flew to her throat. "Hadn't he better resign?"

Her longtime friend shook his head. "Not if you feel equal to what I suggest. To resign would have a bad effect on the nation and a serious effect on the President. He has staked his life on his promise to the world to do all in his power to secure peace. If he resigns, all incentive to recover is gone."

The tea tray arrived. "What do you suggest?"

"His nerves are crying out for rest, and any excitement is torture." Dr. Grayson leaned his elbows on his knees. "Have everything come to you. Weigh the importance of each and see if heads of state can solve them without the guidance of your husband."

The familiar sound of spoon clinking on china afforded Edith time to slow her breathing. "Everything that comes to an executive is a problem."

"He has always discussed public affairs with you so you will not come to them uninformed." Looking weary, Dr. Grayson ran a hand through his hair.

Dolly Madison had once acted as her husband's secretary. According to the doctor, Edith's only option was to serve as President Wilson's representative. She met the doctor's eye. "It shall be my stewardship."

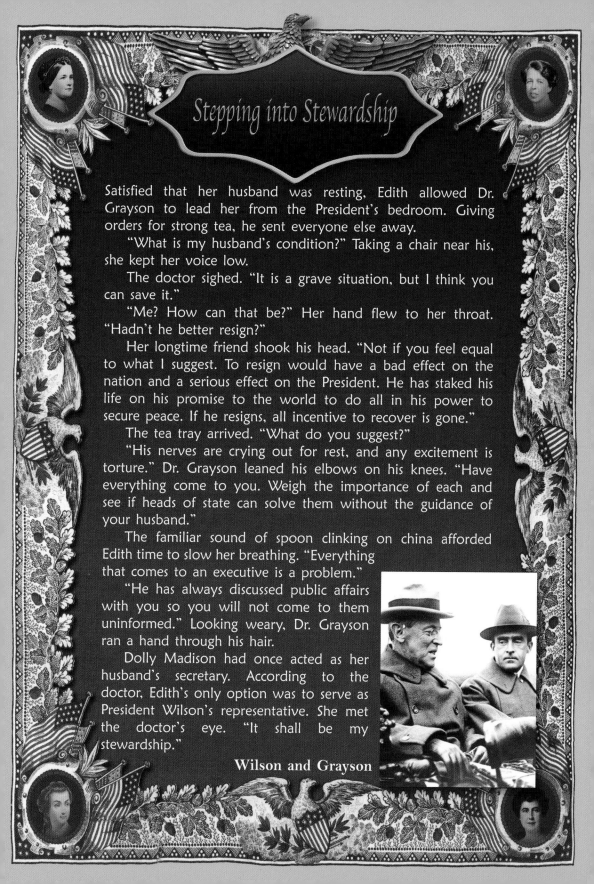

Wilson and Grayson

1840   The Bolling Home at 314 Main Street in Wytheville, Virginia, is built. Edith Bolling Wilson and eight of her ten siblings will be born in this house.

1872   Edith is born the seventh child of William and Sallie Bolling in Wytheville, Virginia.

1914   Ellen Wilson, Woodrow's first wife, dies on August 6. On May 9, President Wilson declares Mother's Day an official national holiday. It will celebrate "our love and reverence for the mothers of our country."

1915   Edith Bolling Galt first meets President Woodrow Wilson in March. In May, German submarines torpedo and sink the British luxury liner *Lusitania*. Many passengers die, including 128 Americans. Edith helps President Wilson compose a firm protest to Germany.

Secretary of State William Jennings Bryan resigns in disagreement with the president's stand on the sinking.

Edith marries President Wilson on December 18 in her Washington, D.C., home. Fifty guests are present, all of them family of the bride and groom.

1916   Even though women are not allowed to vote, Edith is by her husband's side as he campaigns for reelection and wins a second term as the nation's leader.

1917   On April 2, Edith observes from the Capitol gallery as President Wilson asks Congress to declare war on Germany.

1918 In January, President Wilson gives his Fourteen Points speech to Congress.

On November 11 at 3:00 a.m., word reaches Edith and President Wilson that the Germans signed the Armistice and World War I is ended.

Edith and President Wilson sail for France aboard the *George Washington* to lobby for the League of Nations.

1919 The Treaty of Versailles is signed on June 28. It includes an agreement to form the League of Nations.

On September 3, Edith and President Wilson embark on a national train tour to campaign for the League of Nations.

1920 On January 10, the League of Nations is founded. The United States is not a member.

In August, Congress ratifies the right to vote for women.

In December, President Wilson receives the 1919 Nobel Peace Prize.

1924 President Wilson dies on February 3.

1961 Edith rides in the inaugural parade for President John F. Kennedy. She dies on December 28, on what would be her husband's 105th birthday.

Chapter 1. Bishops and Books

1. Edith Wilson, *My Memoir* (New York: The Bobbs-Merrill Company, 1939), pp. 19–20.
2. Ibid., p. 1.
3. Ibid., p. 2.
4. Ibid., p. 1.
5. Ibid., p. 2.
6. Ibid., p. 2.
7. Ibid., p. 3.
8. Ibid., p. 3.
9. Edith Bolling Wilson Birthplace Museum, "The Bolling Home History," http://edithbollingwilson.org/bolling-home/
10. Edith Wilson, *My Memoir* (New York: The Bobbs-Merrill Company, 1939), p. 1.
11. Ibid.
12. Ibid., p. 4.
13. Ibid., p. 5.

Chapter 2. Stories and Cars

1. Edith Wilson, *My Memoir* (New York: The Bobbs-Merrill Company, 1939), p. 13.
2. Ibid., p. 18
3. Ibid.
4. Stephen A. Hansen, *A History of Dupont Circle: Center of High Society in the Capital* (Mount Pleasant, SC: The History Press, 2014), Chapter 3.
5. Carl Sferrazza Anthony, *First Ladies: The Saga of the Presidents' Wives and Their Power 1789–1961* (New York: William Morrow, 1990), p. 325.
6. Ibid., p. 302.
7. Wilson, p. 3.

Chapter 3. Muddy Shoes and Marriage

1. Carl Sferrazza Anthony, *First Ladies: The Saga of the Presidents' Wives and Their Power 1789–1961* (New York: William Morrow, 1990), p. 343.
2. Ibid., p. 351.
3. Ibid.
4. Ibid., p. 352.
5. Ibid., p. 324.

6. National First Ladies Library. http://www.firstladies.org/biographies/firstladies. aspx?biography=29
7. Anthony, p. 351.

Chapter 4. Wilson's Second First Lady

1. Gregory R. Suriano, Editor, *Great American Speeches* (New York: Gramercy Books, 1993), pp. 140–141.
2. American President: A Reference Resource: "Edith Wilson," The Miller Center, http://millercenter.org/president/wilson/essays/firstlady
3. Carl Sferrazza Anthony, *First Ladies: The Saga of the Presidents' Wives and Their Power 1789–1961* (New York: William Morrow, 1990), pp. 360–361.
4. Ibid.
5. PBS: The Great War, World War I Casualties https://www.pbs.org/greatwar/ resources/casdeath_pop.html
6. Edith Wilson, *My Memoir* (New York: The Bobbs-Merrill Company, 1939), p. 221.
7. Anthony, p. 366.
8. Ibid., p. 368.
9. The White House.gov. https://www.whitehouse.gov/1600/presidents/ woodrowwilson

Chapter 5. Mrs. President?

1. Edith Bolling Wilson Birthplace Foundation Museum, http://edithbollingwilson. org/
2. Carl Sferrazza Anthony, *First Ladies: The Saga of the Presidents' Wives and Their Power 1789–1961* (New York: William Morrow, 1990), pp. 372.
3. Anthony, pp. 377–378.
4. U.S. Department of State, Office of the Historian, https://history.state.gov/ milestones/1914-1920/league
5. Anthony, p. 384.

Books

Ashby, Ruth. *Woodrow and Edith Wilson (Presidents and First Ladies)*. New York: World Almanac Library, 2005.

McCallops, James C. *Edith Bolling Galt Wilson: The Unintended President* (New York: Nova Science Publishers Inc., 2003.

Wheeler, Jill C. *Edith Wilson (First Ladies)*. Edina, MN: Abdo Publishing Company, 2009.

Works Consulted

Anthony, Carl Sferrazza. *First Ladies: The Saga of the Presidents' Wives and Their Power 1789–1961*. New York: William Morrow, 1990.

Berg, A. Scott. *Wilson*. New York: G.P. Putnam's Sons, 2013.

Chandler, Michael Alison. "A President's Illness Kept Under Wraps." *The Washington Post,* February 3, 2007. http://www.washingtonpost.com/wp-dyn/content/article/2007/02/02/AR2007020201698.html

Foster, Feather Schwartz. *The First Ladies: From Martha Washington to Mamie Eisenhower, An Intimate Portrait of the Women Who Shaped America*. Nashville, TN: Cumberland House, 2011.

Hansen, Stephen A. *A History of Dupont Circle: Center of High Society in the Capital*. Mount Pleasant, SC: The History Press, 2014.

Klapthor, Margaret Brown. *The First Ladies*. Washington, D.C.: National Geographic Society and White House Historical Association, 1999.

Levin, Phyllis Lee. *Edith and Woodrow: The Wilson White House*. New York: Scribner, 2001.

Ross, Ishbel. *Power with Grace: The Life Story of Mrs. Woodrow Wilson*. New York: G.P. Putnam's Sons, 1975.

Smith, Gene. *When the Cheering Stopped: The Last Years of Woodrow Wilson*. New York: Morrow Publishing, 1964.

Suriano, Gregory R., Editor. *Great American Speeches*. New York: Gramercy Books, 1993.

Wilson, *Edith Bolling Galt. My Memoir.* New York: Bobbs Merrill Company, 1939.

On the Internet
Edith Bolling Wilson, Birthplace Foundation and Museum
    http://edithbollingwilson.org/
The Miller Center: "Edith Wilson"
    http://millercenter.org/president/wilson/essays/firstlady
National First Ladies' Libraries: "Edith Wilson"
    http://www.firstladies.org/biographies/firstladies.aspx?
    biography=29
President Woodrow Wilson House
    http://www.preservationnation.org/travel-and-sites/sites/
    woodrow-wilson-house.html
This Day in History: "Woodrow Wilson Proclaims the First Mother's Day Holiday."
    http://www.history.com/this-day-in-history/woodrow-wilson-proclaims-
    the-first-mothers-day-holiday
The White House: First Ladies: Edith Bolling Galt Wilson.
    https://www.whitehouse.gov/1600/first-ladies/edithwilson
The Woodrow Wilson Presidential Library and Museum
    http://www.woodrowwilson.org

administration (ad-mih-nih-STRAY-shun)—The government officials who work under a president.

aristocracy (ayr-ih-STAH-kruh-see)—Members of the ruling class.

baptize (BAP-tyz)—To welcome someone into the Christian faith by sprinkling or dunking them in water.

bishop (BIH-shup)—A Christian priest who is the head of more than one church.

cabinet (KAB-nit)—The group of people who advise the President, including the Vice President and heads of 15 executive departments: Secretaries of Agriculture, Commerce, Defense, Education, Energy, Health and Human Services, Homeland Security, Housing and Urban Development, Interior, Labor, State, Transportation, Treasury, and Veterans Affairs, and the Attorney General.

catechism (KAT-eh-kism)—A series of questions and answers used to instruct Christians in the principles of Christian religion.

confirmation (kon-fir-MAY-shun)—A religious ceremony that allows a person to become a full member of a church.

courtship (KORT-ship)—The dating period before marriage.

descendant (deh-SEN-dunt)—A person's child or later offspring.

Episcopal (ee-PIS-kuh-pul)—Governed by or overseen by a bishop.

incumbency (in-KUM-ben-see)—Being in a political office.

invalid (IN-vuh-lid)—One who needs to be cared for because of illness or injury.

league (LEEG)—An association between groups or states for the promotion of common interests.

memoir (MEM-whar)—An account of one's personal life and memories.

orchid (OR-kid)—A type of showy flower grown in temperate and tropical regions.

paralyze (PAYR-uh-lyz)—To make someone or something unable to move.

stewardship (STOO-werd-ship)—The responsibility of protecting something.

stroke (STROHK)—A medical event during which a blood vessel leading to the brain is blocked or torn, starving the brain of oxygen. Strokes can result in weakness or paralysis of parts of the body, loss of consciousness, and death.

Treaty of Versailles (TREE-tee of ver-SIE)—Signed June 28, 1919, a peace treaty that ended World War I between Germany and the Allied Nations. (Versailles is a palace near Paris, France.)

yacht (YOT)—A sailing vessel used for cruising or racing.

PeggySue Wells is the award-winning author of two dozen books, including a *USA Today* and *Wall Street Journal* bestseller and audio finalist. Her titles are published nationally and internationally and have been translated into several languages. Radio cohost and mother of seven children, PeggySue visits schools to share the secrets that make reading and writing fun. Visit www.PeggySueWells.com.